Prayers in Praise of God

Prayers in Praise of God

by

Dr. Marian Jackson Patterson

DORRANCE PUBLISHING CO., INC.
PITTSBURGH, PENNSYLVANIA 15222

The opinions expressed herein are not necessarily those of the publisher.

ISBN # 0-8059-6572-6
Printed in the United States of America

First Printing

For information or to order additional books, please write:
Dorrance Publishing Co., Inc.
701 Smithfield Street
Third Floor
Pittsburgh, Pennsylvania 15222
U.S.A.
1-800-788-7654
Or visit our web site and on-line catalog at
www.dorrancepublishing.com

Dedication

For my beloved parents, Marion Charles and Ida May Jackson, in memoriam.

For my cherished children: Edward Levert Patterson, Irene Roberta Patterson Bowdry, and Richard Lloyd Patterson.

Acknowledgment

Scriptural references are to the HOLY BIBLE: NEW INTERNA-
TIONAL VERSION ®. NIV ®. Copyright © 1973, 1978, 1984 by
the International Bible Society. Used by permission of Zondervan.

The "NIV" and "New International Version" trademarks are regis-
tered in the United States Patent and Trademark Office by
International Bible Society.

Contents

Preface

Shortly after I was elected to the position of Elder by the congregation of Park Hills Community Church of the Reformed Church in America (RCA), the pastor appointed me to the position of Liturgist. One of my duties included giving a prayer at the Sunday morning service. Selecting a layperson to serve as Liturgist and to assist in the worship service is a common practice, paralleling the service given by the apostles of Christ in the early Christian church. As a result of this responsibility and a greatly enhanced spiritual life, I wrote *Prayers in Praise of God.*

My professional career included forty-five years as a public school administrator, teacher of mathematics at the high school and college levels in the Los Angeles School District (which later became the Los Angeles Unified School District) and the California State University system, respectively, and mathematician for an aircraft corporation during World War II. In recent years, I received a doctorate from the University of Southern California in Educational Administration and Curriculum.

In researching the subject of prayers, I found that there were few prayers devoted to simply praising God. Therefore, motivated by the results of my research and encouraged by the confidence of our pastor, I decided to write original prayers utilizing the New International Version (NIV) Study Bible as a reference. I was confident this collection of short prayers could become a very reverent and loving part of Christian worship services.

Unlike most Christian prayers that usually begin with adoration and praise prior to acknowledging sins and shortcomings and prior to offering supplications, *Prayers in Praise of God* offers only praise. A prayer of praise to God will grant an assurance that you have God's attention and, as a reward, will promote a more perfect knowledge of God.

Marian Jackson Patterson, Ed.D.
Los Angeles, California
October 2000

Praising God for His Blessings

Comfort

Dear Heavenly Father,

You are the Father of compassion and the God of all comfort. You comfort us in all of life's conflicts and reverses. Whether we are on freeways, airways, or city streets, you are with us. Your rod and your staff they comfort us. Praise your holy name.

You give us comfort and joy instead of sorrow; you turn our unhappiness into gladness. Because of your comfort, we are like a well-watered garden. Praise your holy name.

Just as the sufferings of Christ flow over our lives, so also through Christ our comfort overflows. The comfort you give us is sufficient for this moment, this day, this life. Praise your holy name.

Please accept our prayer of thanks in the name of your Son, Jesus Christ. Amen.

Scripture references (by paragraph)
2 Cor. 1:3; Ps. 23:4
Jer. 31:12-13; Isa. 58:11, 66:13
2 Cor. 1:5

God's Goodness

God of All Goodness and Grace,

You are forgiving and good, abounding in love to those who call you. You have compassion on all you have made. We will celebrate your abundant goodness and joyfully sing of your righteousness. No good thing do you withhold from those whose walk is blameless. Praise your holy name.

O Lord, the earth is full of your goodness. In the morning the splendid sunlight engulfs us in its warmth and beauty. At eventide the luminous stars of night scatter points of light across a darkened sky. Praise your holy name.

The lofty mountains and lush valleys are yours, O God. The sandy shoreline and the depth of the oceans belong to you. Dear God, we cannot take one step or cast one glance without witnessing the truth, goodness, and beauty of the world that you created. You are good, and your love endures forever. Praise your holy name!

This prayer we offer in the name of Jesus Christ, our Lord and Savior. Amen.

Scripture references (by paragraph)
Ps. 84:11, 86:5, 145:7, 9, 150:1-6
Gen. 1:14-18
Ps. 24:1, 100:5, 118:1; Isa. 6:3; 1 Cor. 10:26; Gen. 1:9-10

God's Word

Eternal Father,
    We want to sing your praises and to hear your Word—Words that descend like dew, like showers on new grass, like abundant rain on tender plants. In your Word we will hear your voice and learn your will. Praise your holy name.
    As the rain and the snow come down from heaven and do not return to it without watering the earth and making it bud and flourish, so it is with your Word that goes out. It will not return empty. Your Word is living and active. We will keep your Word in our hearts. Praise your holy name.
    Your Word, O Lord, is flawless. It is a lamp to our feet and a light for our path; it gives understanding to those who will listen. Heaven and earth will pass away, but your Word will never pass away. Praise your holy name.
    Trusting in your Word, we offer this prayer in the name of your Son, our Savior, Jesus Christ. Amen.

Scripture references (by paragraph)
Ps. 9:1-2, 143:10, 150:1-6; Eph. 5:17; Deut. 32:2
Isa. 55:10-11; Prov. 30:5; Heb. 4:12; Deut. 11:18
2 Sam. 22:31; Ps. 119:105; Mark 13:31

Good and Perfect Gifts

God of All Goodness and Grace,

You are the giver of all good and perfect gifts. We celebrate your abundant goodness and rejoice in the bounty of your glorious gifts. Your gifts are irrevocable. Praise your holy name.

You open your hand and satisfy our desires. With love divine, you put everything on earth under man's rule: all flocks and herds, the beasts of the field, the birds of the air, and the fish of the sea. You gave to man every green plant on the face of the earth and every tree. Praise your holy name.

You give each man his own gift: the gift to serve, to teach, or to lead. Different kinds of gifts but the same Spirit; different kinds of service but the same Lord; different kinds of working but the same God. Praise your holy name.

With surpassing grace, you gave us the greatest gift of all–The gift of eternal life in Christ Jesus our Lord. Praise your holy name.

This we pray in the name of our Savior, Jesus Christ. Amen.

Scripture references (by paragraph)
James 1:17; Eccles. 3:13; Ps. 45:7
Gen. 1:26-29; Ps. 8:6-8, 145:16
Ps. 145:16; Rom. 12:6
Rom. 6:23; 1 Cor. 15:55, 9:15; John 3:15-16

Goodness

Dear Heavenly Father,

From the fullness of your grace we have all received one blessing after another. We need no greater proof of your love than the blessings you continually shower upon us. The sunshine and the rain, both in their own way, minister to us. In everything we give thanks, whether the experience is joyful or painful, because, in you, each will become a blessing. You turn sorrow into joy and mourning into a day of celebration. Praise your holy name.

How bountiful are the provisions that you have created for our bodies and souls. You have given us the blessings of material comforts that we, this day, enjoy and spiritual comforts that exceed all the delights of the world. The heavens are yours, and yours also is the earth. You founded the world and all that is in it. We will sing praises continually to declare your wonderful goodness. Praise your holy name.

We humbly offer this prayer for the blessings we have received in the name of our Lord and Savior, Jesus Christ. Amen.

Scripture references (by paragraph)
Esther 9:22; Ezek. 34:26; John 1:15
Ps. 89:11; Eph. 1:3

Grace

God of All Grace and Glory,

We rejoice in the glorious gift of your grace and other blessings without number. Your abundant provision of grace through your Son, Jesus Christ, overflows our meager lives. Praise your holy name.

When we are weak or when we suffer insults, hardships, and difficulties, your grace is sufficient. You turn our weaknesses into strengths, our insults into respect, and our hardships and difficulties into prosperity. Praise your holy name.

Sin shall not be our master, because we are under your grace. Through the riches of your grace you have forgiven us. You have given us peace in a world that is full of turmoil. Praise your holy name.

From the fullness of your grace we have received the greatest gift of all: the indescribable gift of your only Son. Praise your holy name.

Humble in the knowledge that your gift of grace, which reigns through righteousness to bring eternal life to those who believe, we offer this prayer in the name of your Son, Jesus Christ. Amen.

Scripture references (by paragraph)
Ps. 150:1-6; Eph. 1:7; Rom. 6:17
2 Cor. 12:9-10; Heb. 11:34
John 1:16; Rom. 6:14
2 Cor. 9:15
Rom. 6:23

Infinite Goodness

God of All Goodness and Grace,

We come to sing your praise, to speak your word, and to declare your wonderful goodness. Lord, the world and all its peoples are yours. There is no place without you and nothing that does not bear the mark of your creation. Praise your holy name.

The glorious splendor of your majesty is everywhere for us to behold. We come to praise you and to bow our heads in worship. We are grateful for your infinite goodness and humble in the presence of your infinite power. Praise your holy name.

We thank you for the beauty of the earth, for the glory of the skies, and for life in its abundance. We understand that everything we have is because of your infinite goodness. The things you plan for us are far beyond our imagination. Praise your holy name.

Please accept this prayer in the name of your Son, Jesus Christ. Amen.

Scripture references (by paragraph)
Ps. 24:1, 100:3-4; 1 Cor. 10:26
Isa. 6:3; Exod. 15:6-7; Ps. 150:1-6
Eccles. 3:11; Ps. 31:19

Joy

God of All Power and Love,

We rejoice before you, we are glad, and we sing for joy. Each day brings forth a joyous new song from early morning dawn through evening twilight. Praise your holy name.

The roar of the ocean waves proclaims your joy; even the flowers in the garden paint a picture of your joy. The joyousness of your presence is whispered by the breezes in the forest and illuminated by the starry sky at night. Majestic mountains sing together for joy. Praise your holy name.

Your enduring love fills our days. We are humble in your presence as we marvel at the joyousness of the whole earth. Praise your holy name.

We thank you for the joy of your salvation and beg that you accept our prayer in the name of your Son, Jesus Christ. Amen.

Scripture references (by paragraph)
Ps. 5:1, 65:8; Neh. 12:43
1 Chron. 16:32-33; Ps. 8:3, 16:11, 21:6, 98:8, 148:3
Ps. 48:2
Ps. 51:12

Life

Dear Heavenly Father,

We cannot count the good things you have given us, and we rejoice in your gifts. You have given us a life on this earth, but more than that, you have given us eternal life through your Son, Jesus Christ. Praise your holy name.

Our life is not our own. You are our life. You have kept the highest heavens for yourself and given all the earth to man. Even with all the earth, it is not for us to direct our steps but to do your will. Praise your holy name.

You give us strength when we are weary; you give us victory over death. This is more than we could dream. Praise your holy name.

Today as we reverently worship you and rededicate our lives to you, we offer this prayer in the name of our Lord and Savior, Jesus Christ. Amen.

Scripture references (by paragraph)
Rom. 6:23; Ps. 150:1-6; Deut. 30:20
Deut. 10:14; Heb. 10:7; Jer. 10:23; Ps. 115:16
Matt. 22:37; John 13:34
1 Cor. 15:54-55

Peace

God of Love and Peace,

You are peace. Your peace like a river flows over us. Our homes may be broken because of divorce. Our homes may be diminished by the death of a loved one. Our homes may be anxious because of fear. But if our minds are steadfast and we trust in you, you will keep us in perfect peace. Praise your holy name.

The fruit of your Spirit, O Lord, is love, joy, peace, patience, kindness, goodness, faithfulness, gentleness, and self-control. This wealth of riches is all we need. Praise your holy name.

You call us to live in peace with everyone, and you ask that we not take revenge. Vengeance is yours, O God. If we leave room for your wrath, you reward us with joy. Praise your holy name.

Through your Son you proclaimed, "My peace I give you." Now, may this peace, which transcends all understanding, guard our hearts and minds as we offer this prayer in the name of your Son, our Savior, Jesus Christ. Amen.

Scripture references (by paragraph)
Ps. 29:11; Isa. 26:3
Gal. 5:22-23
Rom. 12:18-19; Prov. 12:20
John 14:27; Phil. 4:7

Promise

Dear Heavenly Father,

From the beginning of time you promised the crown of life to those who love you and keep your commandments. You promised eternal life. Praise your holy name.

Even though our promises are fragile, forgotten, and false, your promises prevail forever and ever. Not one word of your promise will fail; every promise will be fulfilled. You are patient with us, not wanting us to perish, waiting for each of us to come to repentance. Praise your holy name.

According to your promise, every stain in our lives is removed. We are given everlasting life and made heirs of your kingdom through the blood of your Son, our Savior and Redeemer. Praise your holy name.

Faithfully believing in your promise, we humbly offer this prayer in the name of your Son, Jesus Christ. Amen.

Scripture references (by paragraph)
Titus 1:2; James 1:12; 1 John 2:25
1 Kings 8:56; Josh. 23:14; 2 Peter 3:9
Eph. 3:6; Gal. 3:29, 4:1-7; Rom. 8:17

Trust

Almighty and Everlasting God,

To you we lift up our souls. Our hearts rejoice for we trust in your holy name. We trust in you though the mountains fall into the heart of the sea and the waters roar and foam. Some trust in material goods and the pleasures of this world, but we trust only in you. Praise your holy name.

We trust that you will still the storm to a whisper, quell our heartaches, dispel our disappointments, and give us peace. When we are afraid, we trust in you. Praise your holy name.

You admonish us to trust in you with all our heart and to lean, not on our own understanding, but in all our ways to acknowledge you. Even though our human minds cannot comprehend your majesty and our human hearts dare not approach your grandeur, we can always trust in you. Praise your holy name.

Trusting fully in you, O God, we offer this prayer in the name of our Lord and Savior, Jesus Christ. Amen.

Scripture references (by paragraph)
Ps. 20:7, 25:1, 33:21, 46:2
Ps. 33:21, 107:29; Prov. 3:5
Job 36:26

Praising God for His Love of Man

Adoration

Lord God, Maker of Heaven and Earth,

We sing joyful songs of your love. Everything you have created is good, and we receive it with praise and adoration. Praise your holy name.

You made the heavens. You made the earth. You sent the sun to brighten the day, and the moon and stars to illuminate the night. Praise your holy name.

You have created things in heaven and on earth, visible and invisible: galaxies in the universe that are too far for our sight and particles on earth that are too small for our seeing. You, alone, perform great wonders. Praise your holy name.

And though we will always be unworthy of your great love, we humbly offer this prayer in the name of our Lord and Savior, Jesus Christ. Amen.

Scripture references (by paragraph)
Ps. 65:8; Gen. 1:31; Ps. 100:1-4
Gen. 1:1; Ps. 8:3, 96:5, 136:5-9
Job 37:14; Col. 1:16
Gen. 32:10; Job 40:5; Luke 17:10

Caring

God of All Goodness and Grace,

We give you praise and adoration. We thank you for caring for us. We are fragile. Our lives are but a breath, our days but a fleeting shadow. Even so, you are mindful of us. Praise your holy name.

No matter how much anxiety we cast on you, you continue to love us and to hold us in your timeless care. You cared for us through our summer experiences of family reunions, Olympic games, picnics, sandy beaches, and lofty mountains. Praise your holy name.

When we make supplication for mercy, it is hard to wait, hard to be patient. We live in darkness and long for light. If we trust in you, your loving care will turn our night into day, our misery into joyous service, and death into life everlasting. You will sustain us. Praise your holy name.

Faithfully trusting in you because you are a caring God, we offer this prayer in the name of your only Son, Jesus Christ. Amen.

Scripture References (by paragraph)
Ps. 144:3-4; Nah. 1:7
1 Pet. 5:7
Ps. 55:22; 2 Sam. 22:29; Isa. 58:10

Faith

Dear Heavenly Father,

We worship you, knowing that you are a faithful God, keeping your covenant of love to a thousand generations of those who love you and keep your commandments. You are a faithful God. Your faithfulness continues through all generations. Praise your holy name.

To the faithful you show yourself faithful. To the blameless you show yourself blameless. To the pure you show yourself pure. You are our lamp, O Lord, you turn our darkness into light. Praise your holy name.

You are just and will not forsake your faithful ones. You admonish us to live by faith, not by sight. You are faithful to all your promises and loving toward all you have made. Praise your holy name.

You have promised that, if we have faith as small as a mustard seed, we can say to a mountain "move," and it will move. Nothing will be impossible for us. Praise your holy name.

In faith we offer our prayer for your eternal praise, honor, and glory in the name of our Lord and Savior, Jesus Christ. Amen.

Scripture references (by paragraph)
Deut. 7:9; Exod. 20:6; Ps. 100:5
2 Sam. 22:26, 29
Ps. 37:28, 145:13
Matt. 17:20
Ps. 111:10

God Is Love

God of All Power and Love,

We bow before you to worship you in humble gratitude for your undeserved and unchanging love. We cannot fathom the height, the breadth, or the depth of your love. It surpasses our knowledge; it exceeds our comprehension. You are love. Praise your holy name.

You are gracious, merciful, faithful, and full of compassion. You are light, and spirit, and holy. You are the builder of everything, the King of all the earth. You are the Lord our God. And you are love. Praise your holy name.

For those who do not keep your commandments, you are a jealous and avenging God, a consuming fire. But for those who love you and keep your commandments, your love is flawless and will never fail. You are love. Praise your holy name.

To you, O God, we offer this prayer in praise of you and your love. We beg that you accept it in the name of your Son, Jesus Christ. Amen.

Scripture references (by paragraph)
1 John 4:8, 16
2 Chron. 30:9; 1 Cor. 10:13; 1 John 1-5, 4:2, 8; Heb. 3:4; Ps. 47:7; Lev. 20:7
Nah. 1:2; Heb. 12:29; 1 John 4:8, 16; Ps. 33:5

God's Love

God of All Power and Love,

Great is your love for those who fear you. Your unfailing love is priceless; it fills the earth. We see your love in the unfolding petals of the rose. We feel your love in the soft warm wind. We hear your love in the robin's song. Praise your holy name.

Your love is better than life. It surrounds us continuously and endures forever. Our senses overflow with the fullness of your love. You give us joy even as we experience sorrow. You show love to thousands of generations that love you and keep your commandments. Praise your holy name.

This we pray in the name of one who loves us with an unfailing love, your Son, our Savior, Jesus Christ. Amen.

Scripture References (by paragraph)
Ps. 103:11, 36:7
Ps. 63:3, 107:1; Exod. 20:6

God's Way

God of All Wisdom and Knowledge,

We want to worship you, to find your way, and to learn more about your will for us that we may live our lives in praise of you. We want to live life your way. We want to know what your will is. Praise your holy name.

Your creation of man is full of wisdom and perfect in beauty. You are righteous in all your ways and loving toward all you have made. Your way is perfect; your way is just. You revive our souls. Praise your holy name.

We are here to be receptive to your will, to follow in your way, to give you all honor and glory. This we pray in the name of your Son, Jesus Christ. Amen.

Scripture References (by paragraph)
Ps. 40:8, 86:11, 143:10; Eph. 5:172
2 Sam. 22:31-33; Ps. 18:30, 119:7-8, 145:17; Deut. 32:4

Hope

Our Gracious, Loving, and Ever-Present God,

Our hope is in your unfailing love. Our hope is in you all day long. You are our help and our shield. Our soul finds rest in you alone. By faith we rest in hope. Praise your holy name.

We put our hope in your word. You have assured us that we who hope in the Lord will have our strength renewed, will soar on wings like eagles, will run and not grow weary, will walk and not be faint. Praise your holy name.

We will be joyful in hope, patient and faithful, confident that you will not abandon us to the grave. We rest on the hope of eternal life, the blessed hope of the glorious appearance of our Lord and Savior, Jesus Christ. Praise Your Holy Name.

Now trusting in that hope, we humbly offer this prayer in the name of your Son. Amen.

Scripture references (by paragraph)
Ps. 33:18, 25:5, 147:11, 33:20, 62:5; Titus 1:2
Ps. 119:74, 130:5; Isa. 40:31
Rom. 12:12; Acts 2:27; Ps. 49:15; Titus 1:2, 2:13

Love Protects Us

O Lord, the Great and Awesome God,

We thank you for the beauty of the earth, for the glory of the skies, and for the golden splendor of each day. You have made every thing beautiful in its time. During fire, flood, and earthquake, you have kept us free from harm. In time of trouble, you have kept us safe. Praise your holy name.

You have dominion over the universe and all the nations of the world. We have no words with which to express the wonder and the worship with which we are filled as we witness your control of the vast universe. O God, we trust in your holy name, and we take refuge in your arms of love. We thank you and praise you for keeping us safe and protecting us so that we may meet today in friendship and in love. Praise your holy name.

You have dominion over the universe and all the nations of the world. You say to the snow. "Fall on the earth," and to the rain shower "Be a mighty downpour." Your breath produces ice, you control the clouds, and you make the lightning flash. You are beyond our reach and exalted in power. Praise your holy name.

Please accept our prayer in the name of your Son, Jesus Christ, who promised to protect, keep, and be with us always, to the very end of the age. Amen.

Scripture references (by paragraph)
Eccles. 3:11, 13
Job 37:14-18, 23; Deut. 33:27
Job 25:2, 37:6, 10, 15; Ps. 22:28
Matt. 28:20; Ps. 18:2, 62:8

Our Unworthiness

God of All Holiness and Power,

We worship you in spirit and in truth. We laud and magnify your name. We sing your praises and strive to speak your Word. Praise your holy name.

We thank you for your grace that is sufficient to keep us in love and peace. We are humbly grateful for your saving grace; we fall prostrate in awe and wonder before your immeasurable greatness. Praise Your Holy Name.

In reverent humility we know that we are not worthy to be in your presence, not worthy to be part of this beautiful universe. You have not dealt with us according to our sins nor rewarded us according to our iniquities. Praise your holy name.

For as high as the heavens are above the earth, so great is your love for those who fear you. As far as the east is from the west, so far have you removed our transgressions from us. Praise your holy name.

Though we are unworthy of your compassion, we offer this prayer in the name of Jesus Christ our Lord. Amen.

Scripture references (by paragraph)
Ps. 118:24 , 150:1-6
2 Cor. 12:9; Eph. 2:5, 8; Heb. 12:28
Ps. 103:10
Ps. 103:12-13

With Love

Dear Heavenly Father,

We pay homage to your majesty, your glory, and your greatness. In grand omnipotence you created the universe with your Word. You said, "Let there be light," and there was light. You said, "Let there be an expanse between the waters," and the sky appeared. You said, "Let the land produce living creatures," and it was so. With your Word you created all that we have. Praise your holy name.

By your Word you created the universe, but man was created with loving care by your hand. You reached down to the dust of the earth and molded man in your image. Man formed, not because of your spoken Word, but because of the loving touch of your hand. Praise your holy name.

With love surpassing all knowledge you designed man. With love you gave him your image. With love you breathed life into his nostrils. The love you have for man is more than we can comprehend. Praise your holy name.

Please accept our prayer in the name of your Son. Amen.

Scripture references (by paragraph)
Gen. 1:3, 6-8, 24
Gen. 2:7, 1:26-27
Gen. 2:7

Praising God for
His Omnipotence

God's Hand

Dear Heavenly Father,

Your hand, O Lord, is majestic in power. Your hand counts the days and the seasons of our lives. Your hand paints the rainbow and scatters the stars. Even the petals of the rose will not open, nor the sparrow fly, without the touch of your hand. All that we have comes from your hand. Praise your holy name.

If we rise on the wings of dawn, if we settle on the far side of the sea, even there your hand will guide us. You will hold us fast. You open your hand and the desires of every living thing are satisfied. Praise your holy name.

Your hand laid the foundations of the earth; your hand spread out the heavens. In the hollow of your hand you measured the waters; with the breadth of your hand you marked off the heavens. Praise your holy name.

Knowing that all strength and power are in your hand, we offer this prayer in the name of your Son, Jesus Christ. Amen.

Scripture References (by paragraph)
Exod. 15:6
Ps. 139:9, 145:16
Isa. 48:12-13, 40:12
1 Chron. 29:12

God's Wonders

God of All Mystery and Wonder,

We lift up our voices to tell of all your wonders and to praise your great and awesome name. You are the origin, support, and destiny of everything that was, is, and ever more shall be. Generations come and generations go, but the earth remains forever. Praise your holy name.

You stretched out the heavens like a tent; you set the earth on its foundation. You hung the moon, scattered the stars in the sky, and made the sun so bright we cannot even look at it. You cause all streams to flow into the sea, yet the sea is never full. You measure the length of our days by sunrises and sunsets; the length of our lives by how often it rises for each of us. Praise your holy name.

O Lord, my God, many are the wonders you have created. The things you planned for us, no one can recount. If we were to speak and tell of them, there would be too many to declare. Praise your holy name.

No one can match your wonders. Everything you created will endure forever; nothing can be added to it, and nothing can be taken from it. Praise your holy name.

As we consider the wonders you have wrought, we humbly offer this prayer in the name of Jesus Christ, our Savior. Amen.

Scripture references (by paragraph)
Deut. 7:21; Eccles. 3:14; Ps. 9:1
Ps. 40:5, 104:2, 5, 8:3; Job 37:21; Eccles. 1:5, 7
Eccles. 3:14

Euer-Present Help

Almighty and Eternal God,

We gather together to hear your Word and to write your law within our hearts. We desire to do your will. Praise your holy name.

You are close to the brokenhearted and save those who are crushed in spirit. You deliver our souls from death, our eyes from tears, and our feet from falling. Praise your holy name.

When we trust in you, O God, you bring us peace in all that we do. In work, school, family, or retirement, you are our refuge and our strength, our ever-present help in times of trouble. Praise Your Holy Name.

Knowing that you are our ever-present help, we offer this prayer in the name of Jesus Christ our Lord. Amen.

Scripture references (by paragraph)
Ps. 40:8, 143:10
Ps. 34:18, 56:13, 66:9; Rom. 6:23; Rev. 7:17
Ps. 46:1

Omniscience

Almighty and Eternal God,

We thank you for creating man in your image and for giving us the promise that you will never abandon the work of your hands. You know each one of us. We cannot flee from your presence. You perceive our thoughts. You know our ways. Before we speak a word, you know it completely. Praise your holy name.

From the height of the heavens to the depths of the ocean, you are there. From early dawn through late night hours, your right hand holds us fast. You turn our darkness into light; darkness is not dark to you. Praise your holy name.

You do for us far more than we can ever know. All of the universe that we have seen cannot compare to that which we have not seen. This knowledge is wonderful, too lofty for us to attain. Praise your holy name.

Please accept our prayer in praise of you, O God, in the name of your Son, our Savior, Jesus Christ. Amen.

Scripture references (by paragraph)
Ps. 139:1-4
Ps. 139:8-12
Ps. 139:6

Our Refuge

Lord God Almighty,

You are our rock in which we take refuge. You are our strength, our shield, and our salvation. We seek refuge in the shadow of your wings, trusting you to protect us and to keep us from harm. Praise your holy name.

This morning we sing for joy because of your love and grace. We sing because of the blessings that you give us. You are always there for those who are in trouble and for those who are oppressed. Praise your holy name.

The flight of a sparrow and the destiny of a man are both held within the palm of your hand. We know you will comfort those who suffer the loss of a loved one through illness, accident, or terrorism. Praise your holy name.

We strive to live in your grace, to make your Sanctuary our dwelling place. We know that your angels are watching over us. This we pray in the name of your Son, Jesus Christ. Amen.

Scripture references (by paragraph)
2 Sam. 22:3, 31; Ps. 46:1, 36:7; Nah. 1:7
Ps. 5:11, 9:9
Matt. 10:29; Ps. 119:76; 2 Cor. 1:5
Ps. 23:6, 84:4, 91:11

Truth

Dear Heavenly Father,

On this day our humble songs rise and swell in adoration of you. We avidly read your holy Word, eager to know the truth and to learn how to live our lives for you. We seek to live in the light of all goodness, righteousness, and truth. Praise your holy name.

We acknowledge that fearing you is the beginning of wisdom and obeying your commandments is the beginning of understanding. Show us your ways, teach us your paths, and guide us in your truth. We want to walk in your truth. Praise your holy name.

There is no hiding from you. Your eyes saw our unformed bodies before birth. You discern our going out and our lying down. You are familiar with all our ways. Praise your holy name.

O Lord, we call on you in spirit and in truth as we offer this prayer in the name of your Son, Jesus Christ. Amen.

Scripture references (by paragraph)
Ps. 9:1-2, 143:10, Eph. 5:9
Ps. 111:10, 25:3, 26:4-5
Ps. 139:16, 3

Praising God: Special Events

Christmas Season

Dear Heavenly Father,

We joyously await the day of your Son's birth. Today in your sanctuary, we make ready our hearts to receive your wondrous gift. Praise your holy name.

We take time to search for your Son and to prepare to humbly offer ourselves as gifts at the manger. Praise your holy name.

Throughout all the festivities of this Christmas season, we are not forgetful of the cross on the darkened hill and the empty tomb in Joseph's garden. We tremble in the knowledge that the Child in the manger will become the Man on the cross—that the Child born to be King will be crucified for our sins. Praise your holy name.

Please accept this prayer of praise and adoration for your love, your love that gave us your only beloved Son, Jesus Christ. Amen.

Scripture references (by paragraph)
Luke 2:4-5
Luke 2:12
Acts 2:23; Luke 24:2
Rev. 5:13; John 3:16

Church Anniversary

Dear Heavenly Father,

You have given us peace through our Lord Jesus Christ and access by faith into the grace in which we now stand, sheltered in your sanctuary. Praise your holy name.

We have come through many toils and trials. But you promised that on a rock you would build your Church and that the gates of Hades would not overcome it. We are standing on that promise. Praise your holy name.

You have given us faith–Faith so that we may be sure of what we hope for and certain of what we do not see. Through faith, patience, and trust, we will move into the future. Praise your holy name.

The hymns sung by the choir and congregation, our tithes and offerings, and the words of instruction, revelation, and interpretation by the minister are but humble gifts for the strengthening of your Church and the glory of your kingdom. Praise your holy name.

We offer this prayer in the name of your Son, Jesus Christ. Amen.

Scripture references (by paragraph)
Rom. 5:2
Matt. 16:18
Heb. 11:1; 2 Cor. 5:7; Rom. 8:25
1 Cor. 14:12, 26

Diversity of Man

(Black History Month)

Dear Heavenly Father,

In celebration of Black History Month, we thank you for incredible diversity in your creation of man. You gave us wonderful differences in personality, talent, culture, and race. Not even our fingerprints are alike; each of us is unique. You rescue us from oppression and violence, for precious is our blood in your sight. Praise your holy name.

Even as we rejoice in our diversity, we know that we share a common bond: You are the Father of all, and we are heirs to your kingdom. We humbly thank you for this promise and for all the other wonders of your universe. Praise your holy name.

You admonished us to love our neighbor as ourselves, because we are all brothers and sisters in Christ Jesus. In obedience to you, we uphold our multicultural family in Jesus Christ with love and acceptance. Praise your holy name.

Now though we are of various nations, tribes, languages, and people, we are of one heart and mouth as we offer this prayer in the name of your Son, Jesus Christ. Amen.

Scripture references (by paragraph)
Ps. 72:14
Gal. 4:7, 3:29
Mark 12:31; Matt. 22:39; 1 Pet. 2:17
Rev. 14:6

Easter

Loving and Compassionate Father,

We come together today to rejoice and to praise your name. The tomb is empty! Your Son has risen from the dead! He is now alive forever and ever. Praise your holy name.

We are overwhelmed in the presence of your unfailing love for fallen man–This wondrous love, this gift of everlasting life. You gave your Son to bear all the guilt of all our sins, past, present, and future. Praise your holy name.

On this day our humble hosannas rise and swell to praise you. You are exalted over all the nations; your glory is above the heavens. Praise your holy name.

Please accept our prayer in the name of your Son, Jesus Christ, who promised to be with us always, to the very end of the age. Amen.

Scripture references (by paragraph)
Ps. 150:1-6; Luke 24:2-3, 6; Matt. 28:6-7
Ps. 36:7, 31:21; John 6:47; Col. 2:13-14
Phil. 2:9-11
Matt. 28:20

Father's Day

Dear Heavenly Father,

We gather together on Father's Day to worship and adore you. You made Abraham the father of many people, the father of many nations, and the father of kings. You made him fruitful. Praise your holy name.

But more than that you created man in your own image. Man is the image and glory of you. Apostle Paul asked man not to cover his head in your Church, that your image not be hidden beneath a covering. Great is this honor and glory that you bestowed upon man. Praise your holy name.

Though fathers may forsake their children, you will never forsake us. No matter how man fails, your love never fails. Praise your holy name.

Since the beginning of time you have known that man would sadden and disappoint you. Yet out of mercy and eternal love, you gave unworthy man your image. You gave so much to man, much more than he could even dream of. Praise your holy name.

Please accept our prayer in the name of your Son, Jesus Christ. Amen.

Scripture references (by paragraph)
Gen. 17:4-6
Gen. 1:26-27; 1 Cor. 11:7; 1 Kings 10:9
Ps. 36:7, 118:14; Gen. 1:26-27, 6:6
Gen. 1:26-27, 6:6

Lent

Loving and Compassionate Father,

During this season of Lent, we are reminded of our mortality. You formed man from the dust of the ground and breathed into his nostrils the breath of life. Man became a living being. Praise your holy name.

You know how we were formed and how unworthy we are. We are made of dust. All come from dust, and to dust all return. Yet you have compassion on those who fear you: a compassion that passes all understanding. For this we are humbly grateful. Praise your holy name.

Ever mindful that you molded us like clay, we beg that you accept our prayer in the name of our Lord and Savior, Jesus Christ. Amen.

Scripture references (by paragraph)
Gen. 2:7
Ps. 103:13-14; Gen. 3:19; Eccles. 3:20
Job 10:9

Mother's Day

Dear Heavenly Father,

Today on Mothers' Day, we come to glorify your holy name. We thank you for selecting a woman to be the mother of your Son. You blessed this woman; no greater honor could any woman have. Praise your holy name.

We thank you for remembering our mothers in your holy Word. You admonish children not to forsake their mother's teachings nor to despise her when she is old. Your holy Word commands children to honor their mother and father. Praise your holy name.

We humbly thank you for the women who naturally or through adoption have been chosen to experience the blessedness of mother-hood and for those who already have crossed the Jordan River. We are grateful to you for all the mothers whose hope in their children burns eternally, whose love is patient and unceasing, and whose travail and long suffering knows no measure. Praise your holy name.

This we pray in the name of your Son, Jesus Christ. Amen.

Scripture references (by paragraph)
Ps. 9:1-2, 150:1-6, 143: 10; Gal. 4:4; Luke 1:46-48
Prov. 1:8, 23:22; Exod. 20:12; Deut. 5:16; Matt. 15:4, 19:19; Eph. 6:2
    Mark 7:10, 10:19
1 Thess. 2:7; 2 Kings 2:7-12; Gen. 3:16

Palm Sunday

Loving and Compassionate Father,

We gather together this Sunday morning in remembrance of the day when your Son rode into the Holy City on a donkey on his way to the Cross. We humbly thank you for sending your only begotten Son to us, who are so unworthy. We are mournful of the fact that the crowds that waved the palms soon would raise their fists and crucify our King. Praise your holy name.

Every good and perfect gift comes from you, O God, and so we take time to thank you for the precious gift of your Son, Jesus. Praise your holy name.

We are mindful of the long road to Calvary. We wear a cross of palm fronds in humility, remembering that Christ was crucified on a heavy wooden cross. Praise your holy name.

And though we will always be unworthy of your great gift of love, the indescribable gift of your only Son, we humbly offer this prayer in his name. Amen.

Scripture references (by paragraph)
Matt. 21:1-9; Rom. 8:3
James 1:17; John 3:16
Matt. 27:35
2 Cor. 9:15; Ps. 107:43; Eph. 2:4

Women's Day

Dear Heavenly Father,

Today on Women's Day, we remember in your holy Word the description of a woman named Ruth. Ruth fulfilled your law with her selfless devotion and self-giving love. Her life was blessed. Through her we know that women of noble character will find favor in your sight. Praise your holy name.

You selected Mary to bring your Son to earth. Blessed was she among women. What greater honor could any woman have than to be the mother of your Son? Praise your holy name.

After the resurrection, you sent an angel to tell Mary Magdalene and the other women who were seeking your Son at the tomb to go and tell the disciples that He was risen. You chose women to report the news that would bring life everlasting to all mankind. Praise your holy name.

And though your apostle, Paul, declared that the head of woman is man, at the same time he affirmed that woman is the glory of man. Only a woman knows how much grace this glory brings. Praise your holy name.

As we offer this prayer in the name of your Son, Jesus Christ, we thank you for including women in the plan for redemption and salvation. Amen.

Scripture references (by paragraph)
Ruth 3:11; Prov. 31:30
2. Gal. 4:4; Luke 1:46-48
Matt. 28:5-8; Luke 1:42
1 Cor. 11:3, 7